The story of Mary Queen of Scots is the tragedy of a woman ruled by her heart rather than her head. Widowed at 18, she returned to a country she could hardly remember, where she was bewitched by her handsome young cousin, Henry Darnley. But their marriage was the first step towards disaster.

IN A FAR COUNTRY

MARY WAS ONLY FIVE WHEN SHE WAS SENT AWAY TO FRANCE. A GLITTERING FUTURE AWAITED HER THERE, WHEN SHE WOULD BE NOT ONLY QUEEN OF SCOTLAND BUT ALSO OF FRANCE

Mansell

👑 *Mary of Guise above shows her daughter, already Queen of Scotland, to Sir Ralph Sadler. Sir Ralph was an envoy from England, sent by Henry VIII with the express purpose of arranging a match between the baby, still only a few months old, and Henry's five-year-old son Edward*

MARY QUEEN OF SCOTS WAS BORN AT THE Palace of Linlithgow in Scotland, on 7 or 8 December 1542. She was the daughter of James V of Scotland and his French wife, Mary of Guise. Within six days her father was dead and she, as his legitimate heir, became Queen of Scotland, a wild and intractable country divided by clan conflicts and wracked by war. As he lay dying, James, hearing the news of his daughter's birth, despairingly said, 'Adieu, farewell, it came with a lass, it will pass with a lass,' referring to the founding of the Stuart dynasty and prophesying its demise.

Mary's father was, by all accounts, a brave and chivalrous man, although given to fierce moods and deep depressions. He possessed a physical magnetism that endeared him to the common people, and particularly to women. He had at least nine illegitimate children, but less luck in wedlock; James's first wife, Madeleine of France, had failed to survive more than a few weeks of the bleak Scottish climate.

The French connection

His second marriage, to Mary of Guise, was very much a political union. She was from a powerful French family and came with a substantial and much-needed dowry. The marriage reinforced the 'auld alliance' between France and Scotland, drawn together against their common enemy, England. Mary of Guise had also been married before and, when she left for Scotland in 1538, she left a small son called Francis behind, in the care of his grandmother.

Two years after their marriage, James's new Queen gave birth to a son, also called James, and ten months later to another boy, Robert. The succession seemed assured. But then tragedy struck – ten days after Robert was born he and his brother died, within a just a few hours of each other. The grief-stricken King plunged into a gloom that was not lifted by the birth of his daughter Mary a year later.

From the start, the infant Queen of Scotland was at the centre of a political storm. Her paternal grandmother, Margaret Tudor, was the elder sister of Henry VIII of England. If Henry failed to produce heirs, Margaret and her successors would inherit the English throne. But this seemed a remote possibility, because Henry had a son, Edward, and two daughters, Mary and Elizabeth. As soon as Mary became Queen of Scotland, Henry saw that this was his chance to unite the two kingdoms. He proposed that Mary

Christopher Wood Gallery/Bridgeman

JACOBVS.QVINTVS.SCOTTORVM.REX ✳
ANNO. ÆTATIS.SVE.
Z 5

MARIA.LOTHORINGIA .ILLVS .IN.SECVNDIS.NVP
TIIS VXOR ✳ANNO ÆTATIS SVE . Z 4 ✥

– when a little older, of course – should marry his son Edward, still a small child himself.

And, indeed, while the pro-English faction held power in Scotland, a formal contract of betrothal between the two was drawn up. But Henry reckoned without the turbulent nature of Scottish politics. Within a short time supporters of France held sway and the marriage was off. Henry was furious. He sent an English army north, which laid waste the south of Scotland. However, it was only after the Scots suffered a devastating defeat in the battle of Pinkie Cleugh that Mary of Guise decided her daughter must leave the country. The danger of her falling into the hands of the English was now too great.

Whisked away from danger

The dowager Queen proposed that Mary be sent to the safety of France. The Scottish Lords made no objection since, in return, France agreed to send 6000 soldiers to Scotland to help in the fight against the English. A further condition of French help was that Mary, when of age, should marry the Dauphin Francis, the eldest son of Henry II of France. And so the Queen of Scotland would also become the Queen of France – a glittering future indeed.

Mary, therefore, set sail for France and a new life at the tender age of five. Her companions on the voyage included an escort of

Scottish lords, a number of servants and her governess, Lady Fleming. Companions nearer her own age were also provided. Four young Scottish girls, all named Mary like herself, went to France with her. Their names were Mary Beaton, Mary Fleming, Mary Livingston and Mary Seton. Two of them had French mothers, just like herself. The four Marys were to share

National Trust Photo Library

♛ *James V and Mary of Guise above had met only briefly before they were married. At first Mary found it difficult to win James's trust, but he thawed as soon as she became pregnant with their first child. High hopes for the future were dashed when their two sons, James and Robert, unexpectedly died. Unfortunately, misery drove the couple apart rather than closer together. By the time Mary was born, relations between the two were distinctly chilly*

'The most perfect child ... I have ever seen'

HENRY II OF FRANCE ON MARY

♛ *Linlithgow Castle left was the traditional setting for the lying-in of Queens of Scotland. Mary's father, James V, had been born there. Mary of Guise was delighted with Linlithgow, claiming that the palace reminded her of the châteaux she had left behind in France. It was here that Mary was born in 1542. And the infant Queen was baptized in the local parish church, St Michael's, which stands beside the castle*

Musée Condé, Chantilly/Giraudon/Bridgeman

LIFE IN FRANCE

The happiest period of Mary's life now began. She was, from the start, received with almost overwhelming pomp, since Henry II of France made it clear that she was to be welcomed not only as a reigning Queen (he called her *la reinette*, or the little queen) but also as his future daughter-in-law. Firework displays, receptions and festivities of all kinds greeted the tiny Queen on her journey to Saint Germain-en-Laye, where the Royal children were in residence.

Nor could anything have been more fulsome than the praise of Mary's childish charm and her pretty looks by both the French Royal Family and her Guise relations. Her grandmother Antoinette of Guise was particularly ecstatic, enthusing to Mary's mother on the child's intelligence and beauty, as well as her graceful and self-assured movements. Equally enchanted, Henry II wrote that Mary was simply 'the most perfect child that I have ever seen'. Clearly, Mary was an attractive, charming girl, docile and naturally feminine, and already displaying those innocent, winning ways that were to captivate so many of her contemporaries in later years.

Mary saw a great deal of her Guise relatives, but she spent most of her time with the children of the King and Queen of France. Her life in the Royal nursery was filled with childish delights and pleasures, for no children were more fussed over or lavished with care than the children of Henry II and his Queen, Catherine de Medici. The sweet-natured Mary soon formed a close

her life in France and, indeed, much of her tragic life thereafter. Also accompanying her on the journey was 17-year-old James Stewart, one of James V's illegitimate sons. In later years he was to be another important player in the dramatic scenario of Mary's life.

Voyage into the unknown

A fleet of French galleys took Mary and her entourage away from Scotland on 7 August 1548. Even now it was feared that the little Queen might be seized by the English. But two weeks later her mother received the welcome news that Mary had landed safely on the coast of France, at Brest. The six-day voyage had passed without incident. It was to be 13 years before Mary returned to her native land.

♛**Above** *Mary in the early 1550s. After her arrival in France, she was equipped with a completely new wardrobe, because it was thought important that she be dressed in finery reflecting her elevated station. As reigning Queen of Scotland, she had precedence over all the children of Henry II except the Dauphin*

♛ *One of the Royal residences regularly visited by Mary was the great château of Chambord on the Loire* right, *which has been described as 'a marvel of Renaissance architecture'. It has over 400 rooms*

Spectrum

👑 *Henry II − surrounded by the knights of the Order of St Michael* left − *and his wife Catherine de Medici* above *ruled over the most glittering court in Europe. However, Catherine always felt her position was insecure − she had none of the bewitching beauty of many of the Court ladies, she was not royal (being a member of the Italian Medici family) and, for ten long years, she was childless. This last she eventually made up for by producing ten children over the last 15 years of her marriage. Catherine came into her own after the death of Mary's husband Francis II, when she became Regent of France during the minority of her second son, Charles IX. She remained a formidable power in the land until her death in 1589*

THE CHATEAU OF SAINT GERMAIN-EN-LAYE

Mary spent a large part of her childhood in the enormous château of Saint Germain. Of all the residences of the French monarchy, the setting of the château of Saint Germain is perhaps the most beautiful. Built to the west of Paris, on a high escarpment overlooking a meandering stretch of the Seine and Paris itself, it is backed by the vast forest of Saint Germain. The château was built by Francis I, the grandfather of Mary's young fiancé, on the site of a medieval fortress. It has a flat roof, on which King and courtiers loved to promenade and enjoy panoramic views of the surrounding countryside.

Work on the new château began in 1539 under the direction of the architect Pierre de Chambiges but, according to one authority, the King 'took such an interest that one could well say that he was the architect'. Francis was a great, perhaps even fanatical, builder; he built the château of Chambord and the palace of Fontainebleau, and rebuilt the Louvre in Paris, quite apart from setting in motion extensive renovations of his other residences

bond with the King's daughter Elisabeth, two-and-a-half years her junior, with whom no doubt she swapped secrets and enthusiasms. In later life, Mary was to treasure the memory of these golden days in the nursery.

It was also in the nursery at Saint Germain that Mary met her intended husband, the Dauphin Francis, who was a year younger than herself. In contrast to her bouncing good health, Francis was a pale, sickly child, but the two quickly became the closest and most loving of

👑 *Catherine de Medici may have been Queen of France but many regarded Diane de Poitiers* right *as Queen in all but name. Soon after the death of her husband in 1531, Henry, then Duke of Orleans, fell violently in love with her, despite the fact that she was 20 years older than he was. It was a love that was to last until the King's death in 1559. When Mary first met her, she was 48 but still beautiful. Diane regularly had the Royal children to stay at her house at Anet* above. *Her favourite motif was the stag, and she was often identified with Diana, the Roman goddess of the hunt*

👑*Below Catherine, Queen of France, and her ladies at table. The luxury and refinement of the French Court set standards all over Europe – standards that more barbarous courts, such as that of James V, found hard to emulate*

friends. It was apparent that Francis rather hero-worshipped his lively companion and Mary responded to his genuine adoration with what was to be life-long devotion (right up to the day of her death she carried a miniature of Francis). Court observers noticed how well the Dauphin and his young bride-to-be got on, and how happily they danced together.

An idyllic childhood

Although the children spent much of the time in the splendid palace of Saint Germain-en-Laye, they travelled very frequently to other Royal residences. They particularly delighted in Blois and Chambord, two fairytale châteaux in the Loire valley, and Anet, the exquisite house built by Diane de Poitiers, the King's cultivated and devoted mistress. Diane genuinely cared for the children, keen to provide a constant round of amusements for her Royal charges.

The children were surrounded by pets, especially dogs and caged birds – at one time no less than 26 dogs were attached to the Royal nursery. All the children had ponies of their own, and for a short period two bears were part of the nursery household, but the cost of keeping them was too great and they were difficult to control. The slightest occasion was a cause for celebration and entertainment. A more pleasurable and carefree childhood can scarcely be imagined.

The French Court was the most magnificent

> ### 'Your daughter is improving and increasing day by day in stature, goodness, beauty, wisdom and worth. She is so perfect and accomplished in all things...'
>
> MARY'S UNCLE IN A LETTER TO MARY OF GUISE

Musée Condé, Chantilly/Giraudon/Bridgeman

MARY OF GUISE

National Galleries of Scotland

Mary's mother was a remarkable woman, even in a century renowned for forceful female rulers. Born in 1515, she was the eldest daughter of Claude, Duke of Guise, and Antoinette of Bourbon. The Guise family was one of the most powerful and ambitious families in France, but not of the Blood Royal. When she married Louis, Duke of Longueville, at the age of 19, her parents were well satisfied with the match. But just three years later Louis died and Mary was left a widow with a small son, Francis. Meanwhile, James V was looking for a wife. He had met Mary in Paris the previous year, at the celebrations of his own marriage to Madeleine, daughter of the King of France. However, within months Madeleine was dead. Now James remembered Mary. She was an ideal choice: she was tall, comely and well bred, would bring a large dowry, and, most important of all, she had proved that she could bear sons. Within two months of Louis' death, negotiations were under way. Initially reluctant to marry again so soon and to leave France and her son, Mary soon began to look forward with anticipation to the challenge of being Queen of Scotland. She had inherited intelligence, courage and political acumen from her Guise relations, qualities that she would need in full measure during the trials to come.

After James's death in 1542, when she was still only 27, she remained in Scotland to protect her infant daughter's inheritance. By 1548 she had manoeuvred herself into a very powerful position. In 1554 she became Regent of Scotland, a title she held until her death in 1560 from a heart ailment. Although doomed to failure, Mary gallantly sought to establish a peaceful administration in the country by following her brother's advice 'to deal in Scotland in a spirit of conciliation, introducing much gentleness and moderation into the administration of justice'

Left *The Dauphin Francis at the age of eight, in 1552. Small and sickly, with chronic respiratory problems, he must have made a strange contrast to the tall child, blooming with health and over a year older than himself, who was destined to become his wife. Many blamed his poor health on the various potions and medicines of dubious origin that his mother Catherine had taken, first in order of conceive, and then to ensure a successful birth. Francis became King unexpectedly, at the age of 15, when his father was killed in a jousting accident. A year later he died himself, perhaps not so surprisingly, from an ear infection that affected his brain and killed him*

in Europe. It was expected of a French nobleman that, as well as being skilled at the hunt and in the arts of war, he should be able to dance gracefully, play on the lute, write sonnets and converse wittily and knowledgeably on a variety of subjects. No less was expected of his sisters and wife. Diane de Poitiers was an outstanding example of the Renaissance ideal. Famous as much for her intelligence as for her legendary beauty, she was very well read and delighted in the company of poets, painters and musicians.

Golden days at Court

A courtier's life was filled with activities. By day hunting, tournaments, picnics and excursions took place, and in the evenings soirées, masques and balls added further pleasures. This refined and luxurious ambience was the world Mary observed as a child and the one in which she assumed she would live when grown up.

Mary spoke only Scots when she arrived in France. Although she never lost her facility for this 'barbarous and ill-sounding' tongue, she quickly learned to speak French, and French was the language that she naturally spoke and wrote for the rest of her life. The education of the Royal children was taken seriously. Mary was a bright child with an eager willingness to learn. She became familiar with Latin and Greek, as well as English, Italian and Spanish. She learned to draw, sing, play the lute and dance – a skill at which she excelled. It is reported that at the age of 12 she recited a Latin speech of her own composition in front of the whole Court.

An apt and diligent pupil, Mary won the praises of her watchful family. One of her uncles wrote to her mother: 'Your daughter is improving and increasing day by day in stature, goodness, beauty, wisdom and worth. She is so perfect and accomplished in all things...The King has taken so great a liking to her that he spends much of his time chatting with her, sometimes by the hour together; and she knows how to entertain him, with pleasant and sensible subjects of conversation, as if she were a woman of five-and-twenty.' Mary was already set to be the brightest star in the constellation of the French Court.

The golden boy

Henry Stuart, Lord Darnley, born in 1545, was the son of Matthew Stewart, Earl of Lennox, and Lady Margaret Douglas. Lady Margaret was the daughter of Margaret Tudor (Henry VIII's elder sister) by her second marriage to the Earl of Angus. Henry was born and brought up in

By Gracious Permission of HM the Queen

Mansell

♛ *Margaret, Countess of Lennox* left, *was a a very ambitious woman. As a granddaughter of Henry VII, there was a chance that she, or one of her sons, might one day inherit the English Crown from the childless Elizabeth. Her two boys Charles and Henry (Lord Darnley)* above *were six and 17 respectively when Hans Eworth painted this picture in 1563. Both died young, but not before they had fathered children. Darnley and Mary's son was James VI of Scotland and Charles left a daughter, Arbella. If Elizabeth repudiated Mary and her heirs, Arbella Stuart would become Queen, so either way one of Margaret's grandchildren would sit on the throne of England. In the event it was James who became King of England in 1603*

England, where his rebellious Scottish father took up residence after siding with the English against the Scots in 1544.

On Henry's father's side, the Lennox-Stewarts were among the 'royal' noblemen of Scotland, being descended from James I. His mother was even more 'royal', since she was a first cousin of two Queens of England, Mary and Elizabeth. Darnley was thus a contender in the English succession, although at the time of his birth not a close one. He was also a cousin of Mary Queen of Scots. Darnley therefore had the Royal blood of both Scotland and England in his veins and might be called a 'princeling'.

As the eldest of the two sons of the marriage, Darnley was the focus of his parents' ambitions. There is no doubt that he received an education befitting a distinguished nobleman. He learned Latin and possibly Greek, as well as how to ride, hunt and dance. At the age of eight the precocious boy sent 'a little plot of my penning' to Queen

♛Right *This tapestry, embroidered in France in the mid-16th century, shows French noblewomen engaged in one of their favourite occupations: needlework. Some of the work was so intricate that they needed magnifying glasses to see the tiny stitches. The beautiful background pattern is called* mille fleurs

Mary Tudor, no doubt at the suggestion of his doting parents. He was the author of a number of competent and agreeable poems. It is even claimed that it was he who translated the works of Valerius Maximus from Latin into English.

Great expectations

Darnley also had the advantage of remarkable good looks. He was a tall, slender young man with golden hair and a very handsome face. From an early age, however, Darnley was made all too well aware of his illustrious lineage. He was spoiled and indulged, and as a result became entirely self-centred and selfish. This only enhanced his air of self-importance and further encouraged his mother and father to believe that a great future awaited their son.

Thus, while his older cousin was beginning to captivate the French Court with her charm and gaiety, Darnley was being nurtured and groomed for kingship by his zealous parents. But their ambition was to lead to tragedy.

Musée Cluny, Paris/Giraudon/Bridgeman

Royal Cousins

Robert I of Scotland
(Robert the Bruce)
(1274-1329)

Henry VII of England m. Elizabeth of York
(1457-1509)   (1465-1503)

James IV   Margaret Tudor   Archibald Douglas,   Henry VIII
of Scotland m.(1) (1489-1541) m.(2) Earl of Angus   of England
(1473-1513)   (d.1556/7)   (1491-1547)

Mary of Guise m. James V of Scotland   Lady Margaret Douglas m. Matthew, Earl of Lennox   Elizabeth I
(1515-1560)   (1512-1542)   (d.1578)   (1516-1571)   of England
                                                                                                (1533-1603)

James   Robert
(d.1541)   (d.1541)

James Hepburn,   Francis II,   Mary   Henry Stuart,
Earl of Bothwell m.(3) King of France m.(1) Queen of Scots m.(2) Lord Darnley
(c.1536-1578)   (1544-1560)   (1542-1587)   (1545-1567)

James VI of Scotland   m.   Anne of Denmark
and I of England   (1574-1619)
(1566-1625)

Henry   Elizabeth   Charles I   + four who died
(1593-1612)   (1596-1662)   (1600-1649)   in infancy

During her stay in France, Mary came to be known as *la reine blanche* – the white queen – because she so often wore that colour, perhaps because she thought it best set off her vivid colouring. Later on she continued to do so – an inventory of her dresses taken at Holyrood shortly after her return to Scotland lists ten white dresses and many white accessories. These were most often worn with black gowns such as the richly embroidered one *below*

The artist of this watercolour sketch *below right* has greatly softened the rather severe lines actually worn by the Queen of Scots in the 16th century. In fact, were it not for the open skirt, the woman in the sketch could easily be mistaken for a woman of the first half of the 19th century. The artist has also softened her appearance, giving Mary the large doe eyes considered beautiful in his time, instead of the rather small eyes she actually possessed

'THE WHITE QUEEN'

Mary always had a tremendous interest in clothes. As a child during her stay in France she demanded gowns as elaborate as the French Princesses she was raised with, and later on she delighted in dressing up, in Scottish national dress or as a man. She sometimes used clothes in unorthodox ways to make statements about her state of mind, for example wearing black when she wed Darnley. But perhaps the best example of this was the outfit she chose – weeks in advance – for her execution, to demonstrate just how regal a Queen could be, even at such an extreme moment

Ronald Weir/Duke of Atholl

Mary Evans Picture Library

Stuffed shoulder-
wings are sewn
around the armhole,
emphasizing the
horizontal line of
the shoulders

MA= RIA.

Regina   Scotia.

♔ In this miniature by Nicholas Hilliard painted about 1578 *above*, Mary is wearing her traditional black and white. By this time the ruff has turned into a starched lace collar. On her head Mary wears an *attiffet*: a headdress which forms an arc on both sides of her forehead and is covered with a veil dipping over the brow

♔ Mary did not always wear black and white − she loved bright colours such as yellow, blue, green and orange. The richly jewelled gown *left* is slashed on the bodice and sleeves and has an open skirt, revealing contrasting fabric. Underneath she is wearing a farthingale − a sort of crinoline of stiff linen with a hoop of whalebone around the waist, making the skirt stand out around the hips

Under the bodice Mary
wears a vasquine, a sort
of padded corset which
flattens the bust and
accentuates the
slenderness of the waist

Gown is studded with
rubies at neck and
on sleeves, and with
vertical rows of
pearls on bodice,
sleeves and overskirt

FAREWELL TO FRANCE

WIDOWED BEFORE HER 18TH BIRTHDAY, MARY RETURNED SADLY TO SCOTLAND, HER CROWN IN PERIL AND HER FATE UNSURE

👑 With her slightly pointed nose and dark, mysterious eyes, Mary left was a far from conventional beauty, but her colouring was particularly lovely in that she had wonderfully white, smooth skin and abundant, glowing chestnut hair. Her most remarkable physical characteristic, however, was her height, for Mary was about 5 feet 11 inches tall in an age when neither men nor women reached great stature; she was renowned for her graceful, slender and regal bearing. That her husband Francis II, a year her junior, was still very much a child while his wife was blossoming into an attractive young woman is most evident in the famous miniature portrait of the two of them from the book of hours of Catherine de Medici far right. On the coin showing the heads of Mary and Francis above, this difference is tactfully disguised. After her childhood spent at the Paris Court, Mary remained a Frenchwoman in her tastes throughout her life. Below Noblemen and women engaged in forms of dancing that Mary made popular at the Scottish Court when she returned from France

Fotomas. Left:By Gracious Permission of HM the Queen

B Y THE TIME OF HER MARRIAGE TO FRANCIS, IT was clear that Mary was a bewitching young woman. 'In her fifteenth year, her beauty began to radiate from her like the sun in the noontide sky,' wrote the courtier and chronicler Brantôme. Yet this legendary beauty is not so obvious from her youthful portraits. Perhaps what painters failed to capture was the radiance and charm that she obviously possessed – transformed into beauty in the eye of the beholder. One such was the poet du Bellay, who wrote: 'Rest content, oh you mine eyes! Ne'er will you see again so lovely a thing.'

Betrothal and marriage

Mary was not only very attractive, she was also a cultivated young woman who danced, hawked and hunted with exceptional skill and had a genuine love and sympathy for the arts and poetry. By the time she was old enough to be married, she was exactly what she had been trained to be – the most beautiful and accomplished Queen at the most sophisticated court in Europe.

By contrast with his fiancée, the Dauphin was frail and wizened and suffered from a chronic respiratory infection that had afflicted him since birth. Concern for his health was as much the reason for this teenage marriage as any political consideration.

After a formal betrothal on 19 April 1558, the young couple were married in Notre Dame

Louvre, Paris/©RMN

Hic pudor, hic morum probitas hic aulica suada,   *Et lepor, & vita generosa modestia glisčit.*   *Quid mirum, divas ultrò si dia sequantur.*

on 24 April; Mary was all of 15, her husband only 14 years of age. Mary, dressed in a gown of white embroidered with rich and sumptuous jewels, was led to the altar by Henry II. It was an unorthodox choice since white was traditionally the colour of mourning for queens of France, but it was Mary's favourite colour and one she wore often during the rest of her life. Around her neck were precious diamonds and on her head a golden crown studded with pearls, rubies, sapphires and other precious stones. 'She appeared,' wrote Brantôme, 'a hundred times more beautiful than a goddess.'

After the ceremony, the bride and groom passed through the streets of Paris – Mary in a golden coach with her mother-in-law, Catherine, Francis following on horseback – to thunderous applause from the people.

Splendour and illusion

For the first few months of her marriage Mary was ecstatically happy; never before had she been the centre of so much attention, wealth and ceremony; she was now not only Queen of Scotland but the wife of the most distinguished Crown Prince in Europe.

Nevertheless Mary's teenage years at the glittering French Court were tinged with the sense of unreality that colours every subsequent episode in her chequered and tragic life. Her marriage to Francis was probably never consummated, for it is unlikely that the Dauphin reached puberty before he died. But this sullen young man was a devotee of other physical activities,

♛ *Mary's father-in-law, King Henry II of France* above, *was a grim, melancholy man, but he relied on the support of the House of Guise and rewarded its members generously. He appears to have been fond of Mary, unlike his wife Catherine de Medici, who saw her as a rival at court. The tournament* right *at which Henry received fatal injuries was held on 30 June 1559 and was to celebrate both the peace treaty that had just been signed with Spain, and two Royal betrothals, that of his daughter Elizabeth to Philip II of Spain and that of his sister Margaret to the Duke of Savoy. In the course of the jousting Henry was struck on the temple by a lance; he died in Paris ten days later*

Fine Art Photographic Library

♛ *The court chronicler Brantôme touchingly described Mary's desperate unhappiness at leaving France* above*: 'Standing on the stern, close to the rudder, and leaning on the taffrail, Queen Mary wept as she looked at the harbour and the country from which she was departing… repeating plaintively, 'Farewell France! Farewell France! I fear I shall never see you more'*

notably hunting, and he would ride with Mary whenever his health permitted. He clearly adored his beautiful and vivacious wife. She in turn found it easy to be generously affectionate with the boy who had been a comforting and dear friend since her childhood.

Three times a queen

In November 1558, Mary Tudor died and Elizabeth I succeeded to the English throne. In the eyes of Catholic Europe, Elizabeth was illegitimate,

having been born to Henry VIII while his first wife was still alive, and Mary was the rightful successor to the throne of England and Ireland.

The following year Henry II died after suffering injuries in a tournament and Francis and Mary became King and Queen of France. A seal from early in their reign shows Francis and Mary sitting beneath a royal canopy with sceptres and orbs in their hands: the inscription proclaims, 'Francis and Mary by the grace of God, King and Queen of France, Scotland, England and Ireland.'

The turning-point

For Mary, this glory was shortlived. In June 1560 Mary of Guise died and in the following month Elizabeth I, having successfully challenged and defeated the French in Scotland, negotiated the Treaty of Edinburgh, which recognized Elizabeth's right to the throne and banished French troops from Scottish soil. In November of the same year, Francis's health suddenly deteriorated as a result of an inflammation of the ear. Within a short time the infection had spread to the brain and the King was dead at the age of 16, after a reign of just 17 months.

Mary was now no longer Queen of France, nor had she any claim on the English throne. In that same year Scotland had, by Parliamentary decree, enthusiastically embraced the Protestant religion. This did not augur well for the 17-year-old widow who at that point decided to return to her homeland. On 14 August 1561, accompanied by a few distinguished noblemen and her inseparable companions, the four Marys, she set sail

JOHN KNOX

John Knox was responsible, almost single-handed, for the establishment of the Protestant religion in Scotland. A great leader and organizer, he was also a persuasive and popular preacher. Having zealously embraced Calvinism, he used Old Testament wrath to rage against 'papish idolatry' and pleasure of any kind.

When Mary insisted on practising her own religion in the privacy of her chapel, Knox preached against her and organized protests outside the Palace of Holyrood. After one such protest, which had nearly turned into a riot, Mary summoned Knox before her in the vain hope of coming to some understanding. Mary acquitted herself well at first, showing 'shrewdness beyond her years' in challenging Knox over his book *The First Blast of the Trumpet against the Monstrous Regiment of Women*. In this Knox all but denies the right of women to wield any kind of authority. But the interview ended with Mary humiliated and in tears, Knox triumphant and unrepentant

Towneley Hall Art Gallery & Museum, Burnley/Bridgeman

'She appeared a hundred times more beautiful than a goddess'

A COURTIER ON THE BRIDE

♛ The most famous of the many pictures of Mary painted by the court artist, François Clouet, was known as the 'white mourning' portrait below. White was the traditional mourning colour worn by women of the French Royal Family, and it is thought that this picture must have been painted in 1559, the year when Mary was in mourning for her father-in-law, Henry II

for Scotland. There she found a country ravaged and plundered by the English and reduced to appalling poverty; after the luxury and refinement of the French court, it was as if she had stepped back in history at least 100 years.

The first three years of Mary's life in Scotland were relatively uneventful. She surrendered the reins of government to her half-brother Lord James Stewart (now Earl of Moray) and Maitland of Lethington, who ruled prudently and well. Mary meanwhile set about creating a little

corner of France in Scotland.

The round tower of the Palace of Holyroodhouse was refurbished in the French style to house her library, pictures, tapestries and furnishings, and she introduced such refined French entertainments as masques, verse-reading, puppet-shows (a new fashion from Italy) and music-making to the gloomy Scottish evenings. Mary herself was a fine player on both the lute and the virginals and she took particular delight in dancing, often 'beyond midnight', according to the censorious John Knox.

Personal magnetism

In the Scottish countryside Mary found endless opportunities for the hunting, hawking and riding she had so enjoyed in France. She also had archery butts set up in her private gardens at Holyrood and played at golf and pall-mall. Her youthful enthusiasm for such natural pleasures endeared her both to the ordinary people and the nobles, for she brought a ray of sunshine and joy to her austere and gloomy homeland. Her personal appeal seems to have been remarkable. Even one of her sworn enemies, Robert Campbell, reported in 1561 that she had 'an enchantment by which all men are bewitched'.

Mary herself once wrote, 'I do not know how to disguise my feelings,' and perhaps it was her natural warmth and spontaneity that drew people to her. Quite unconsciously she exuded a subtle sensuality that was fatally alluring to the young and romantic. Thus the innocent Mary attracted a number of passionate admirers, among them a young poet called Châtelard who was twice discovered hiding in the Queen's bedchamber. For practical as well as political reasons, Moray and the Scottish lords decided that it was time she remarry.

Mary knew as well as anybody that royal marriages were political unions, not love

The young poet Châtelard seen here singing to Mary in her private chamber above was twice discovered hiding in the Queen's bedchamber. Although Mary had in no way encouraged this hapless young man, once the incidents were made public his execution was inevitable. When, after the Châtelard affair, it was decided that Mary needed a husband, Elizabeth I suggested Robert Dudley, Earl of Leicester below right

Prado, Madrid/Bridgeman

DON CARLOS

As early as her widowhood in France, Mary had considered Don Carlos, heir to the Spanish throne, as a potential husband. The reasons for her choice were purely dynastic. Don Carlos himself was an even more pathetic creature than Francis II. He was physically stunted, weighing less than five and a half stone, with one shoulder higher than the other. He also had a pronounced speech impediment and suffered from epilepsy.

At the age of 17 he fell down a flight of stairs (allegedly in pursuit of a serving maid). For some time after the accident he was blind and partially paralyzed. Then a piece of his skull was removed by drilling, which led to an improvement in his condition but left him susceptible to fits of homicidal mania. Later he developed a passion for his stepmother Elisabeth, the French Princess with whom Mary had been brought up

matches, and she was content to leave the bargaining to Moray. An important consideration of any match was the approval of Elizabeth, who held the promise of the English succession over the Scottish Queen's head.

The marriage market

Front-runner in the marital stakes was Don Carlos of Spain, until Elizabeth made it clear that if Mary accepted a husband of Royal blood from Austria, France or Spain, this would be interpreted as an 'unfriendly act'.

But as hopes faded on that front, another contender entered the stakes: Mary's cousin, Henry, Lord Darnley, then a young man of 19. He and Mary had met once, when, at his mother's insistence, he had gone to France along with other courtiers to present his condolences to Mary on the death of Francis. It is doubtful whether he was singled out for any particular attention by Mary on that sad occasion, but the next time she met him, her curiosity would be aroused in a way that no man had ever aroused it before. Not only did Darnley give the impression of an urbane, cultured man of the world, he was also tall and strikingly handsome, the very antithesis of the poor late Francis.

National Portrait Gallery, London

HOLYROOD

The Palace of Holyroodhouse was begun by Mary's grandfather James IV, who wanted a Royal palace in Edinburgh worthy of his English bride, Margaret Tudor. Many additions have been made since then, though few exterior alterations date from Mary's own reign. She was more concerned about adding a little French style and comfort to the gloomy interiors

♔Detail of the elaborate stonework on the fountain in the forecourt of the Palace *below*. The fountain was copied on the orders of Queen Victoria from an original at the Palace of Linlithgow, where Mary Queen of Scots was born

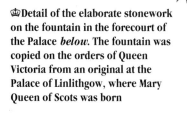

Edinburgh Photographic Library

By Gracious Permission of HM the Queen

♔*Above* The Palace of Holyroodhouse gives the impression of a French château rather than a Scottish or English palace. Much of the building we see today dates from the reign of Charles II, who turned the Palace into a kind of memorial to his Stuart ancestors. Like many places associated with the House of Stuart, the Palace had been knocked about a bit by Cromwell during the Civil War. Of the two towers on the front of the building, the one on the left is the original tower built by Mary's father, James V. The second was added by Charles's architect, Sir William Bruce, to create a symmetrical façade

By Gracious Permission of HM the Queen

♛The ruins of the original Abbey Church of Holyrood *left*. The Abbey was founded in 1128 during the reign of King David I, and the Palace begun as an enlargement of its hospice or guest house. In the 1540s, during the wars known as the 'Rough Wooing', the Abbey suffered terrible damage at the hands of the English troops

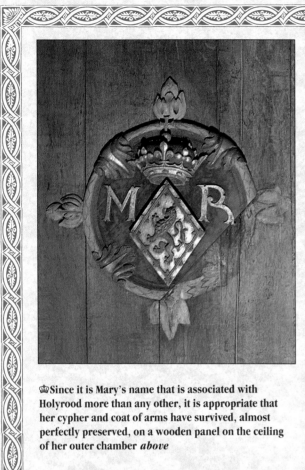

♛Since it is Mary's name that is associated with Holyrood more than any other, it is appropriate that her cypher and coat of arms have survived, almost perfectly preserved, on a wooden panel on the ceiling of her outer chamber *above*

♛The Royal bedchambers in the old part of the building: *above* Mary's own chamber; *left* Darnley's, both restored to something resembling their original state. Very few of the original furnishings have survived, but the rooms do give a rough idea of how the Queen and her consort might have lived. The ceiling in Mary's room is original, though the floor was lowered during the restoration of the Palace in the 17th century to make the room conform with the more gracious and spacious style of the reign of Charles II. Mary would certainly have had panels covered with Flemish woven tapestries of classical and biblical scenes like those on the walls of her chamber. An inventory of the Palace made during her reign lists 88 such panels, many of them brought over from France by her mother, Mary of Guise

♛Something of the atmosphere of gloom that must have pervaded the Palace when Mary returned from France to live there in 1561 can still be felt when one stands at the foot of the Great Stairs *above*

♛The Palace is still used on occasion by the Royal Family when they visit Edinburgh. The rooms in the Royal Apartments, such as the Morning Drawing-room *left*, are furnished with far greater luxury than anything poor Mary would have known. The rich plaster ceilings and magnificent wooden panelwork date from the restoration carried out by William Bruce for Charles II

A FATAL PASSION

MARY FELL DESPERATELY IN LOVE WITH THE HANDSOME DARNLEY AND, DESPITE OPPOSITION FROM ELIZABETH, WED HIM. BUT DISILLUSIONMENT QUICKLY SET IN

AS A POTENTIAL HUSBAND, LORD DARNLEY had two distinct disadvantages as far as the Scots were concerned. He was a Roman Catholic and, to all intents and purposes, was approved of by the English Queen – although why it is difficult to understand.

Elizabeth may have thought that Mary would not take the Darnley match seriously, for it seems curious, if not inexplicable, that she should promote a union between two claimants to her English throne. Perhaps she thought that it was preferable to marriage with one of the great houses of Europe, or perhaps she was just stalling for time, hoping to keep Mary single as long as possible. Whatever her reasons, Darnley went to Scotland in February 1565. Seven days after first setting foot on Scottish soil he met Mary. Her response was instantaneous. She declared that he was 'the properest and best proportioned long man' that she had ever seen.

By Gracious Permission of HM the Queen

⚜Mary, meeting Darnley at Wemyss Castle in Fife below, found him an agreeable companion. By comparison with the rough and unsophisticated Scottish lords, he was handsome, civilized and urbane. He had style – a quality notably lacking in Scottish circles, and one which Mary had rarely seen since her days in France. Small wonder that she delighted in his courtly manners and artistic accomplishments far left. But besides his talents, Mary was enchanted by his physical charms. When she asked Elizabeth for permission to marry Darnley, the English Queen, in a fit of rage, threw his mother – Margaret Douglas, Countess of Lennox right – into the Tower

Edinburgh Photographic Library

Fine Art Photographic Library

Thereafter Darnley hardly left her side.

As the Court began to watch the relationship develop, Darnley caught measles. Mary barely left his bedside, and in the intimacy of the sickroom fell hopelessly and passionately in love with him. No doubt the attraction was a physical one: Mary's sexual feelings had hardly been aroused in her marriage, and in her 22 years she had had no amorous dalliances. The tumultuous rush of emotion she experienced must have been overwhelming.

Now political considerations did not matter a jot. Moray and Maitland could do nothing to dissuade Mary from her infatuation; nor could her Guise relations. The English Ambassador described Darnley's effect on Mary as nothing short of witchcraft.

It was clear that Mary meant to marry Darnley, and she asked Elizabeth's permission, quite confident that it would be given. But to her surprise Elizabeth was furious, claiming that the marriage represented a renewed attempt on

Mansell

⚜ *James Stewart, Earl of Moray, was Mary's illegitimate half-brother above. He, too, was against the match. But Mary did wed Darnley, and Moray was conspicuously absent from the wedding. Within a week he rebelled against the Queen and gathered about him 1200 Protestant lords who marched on Edinburgh. When she heard of Moray's rebellion, Mary right courageously mounted her horse and, with Darnley in gilt armour by her side, defeated the rebels, who were forced to flee*

Mary's part to acquire the English throne. However, Mary was defiant. Elizabeth's adviser wrote, 'There was no point in exercising any persuasion and reasonable means any further.'

Without waiting for the papal dispensation that was necessary when cousins wed, Mary married Darnley at Holyrood on 29 July 1565. On this occasion, she wore not dazzling white but a mourning gown of black. She wanted to show that she had not lightly forgotten her first husband and that, as a widow, her decision to remarry was based on mature reflection. Moreover, she declared that henceforth Darnley was to be known as King Henry. Only after the ceremony and the celebration of Mass did Mary allow herself to don festive clothes and join the rejoicings which, as John Knox sourly commented, 'went on for four days and four nights'.

During the first few weeks of their marriage, Mary could not do enough for Darnley. Openly and impulsively showing her affection for him, she showered him with gifts – a horse, a number of small, precious objects and the right to rule Scotland by her side. The English Ambassador

> ***'No woman of spirit would make choice of such a man that was liker a woman than a man, for he was lovely, beardless and lady-faced'***
>
> SIR JAMES MELVILLE ON DARNLEY

wrote: 'All honour that may be attributed unto any man by a wife, he hath it wholly...No man pleaseth her that contenteth not him; and what may I say more? She hath given over unto him her whole will, to be ruled and guided as himself best liketh.'

Darnley, however, was not much interested in the process of government. Driven by pride and conceit, he would assume dictatorial airs in Council, and then disappear for days on end, hunting, hawking and drinking with his companions, leaving important documents unsigned and affairs of state in abeyance.

Disenchantment sets in

By the beginning of December Mary knew she was pregnant, but this did not increase her affection for Darnley, already starting to wane in the face of his unreasonable behaviour. He had publicly humiliated her, on one occasion causing her to burst into tears, although he had shown her little consideration at the best of times. Most of his courtiers regarded him as an object of derision, since he was by turns foolish, vain, impudent and ungrateful.

Disenchanted with her husband, whose debauched and roistering parties were now the talk of Edinburgh, Mary turned for solace and counsel to David Rizzio, her 32-year-old Italian

Hawkley Studios/National Trust Photographic Library

THE FOUR MARYS

From her childhood up to her marriage with Darnley, Mary's closest attendants were the famous Marys: Livingston, Fleming, Beaton and Seton. All were from noble Scottish families and, like their mistress, all were educated in France. As the Queen's maids of honour and intimate friends, they held a privileged position in the Royal household and, like Mary Stuart, made an impact on the Scottish Court with their charm and beauty. Mary Livingston was a high-spirited and vivacious girl; Mary Fleming 'the flower of the flock'; Mary Beaton the most classically beautiful; while Mary Seton, the most devoted of the Marys, never married but followed her mistress into captivity in England.

The Four Marys are immortalized in a ballad by Sir Walter Scott and are thought to be the 'pretty maids all in a row' in the nursery rhyme traditionally held to be about Mary Queen of Scots, 'Mary, Mary, quite contrary'

♛ *Only months after her wedding, Mary was being serenaded by David Rizzio rather than by her richly clad husband, who turned away from the scene in anger below. Mary had much in common with Rizzio, who was formerly her court musician: despite being of humble birth, he was a skilled poet, finely educated and adept at handling state papers. The two used often to play cards until the small hours*

secretary. Regarded as an upstart by the nobility and as a papal agent by the extreme Protestants, Rizzio now incurred the jealousy of the unstable and possessive Darnley. Soon yet more poison was poured into the open wound of Darnley's jealousy by those Scottish lords who suggested that Rizzio was the Queen's lover.

Feeling himself dishonoured, Darnley entered into a conspiracy with the Protestant lords to overthrow the authority of his wife. He promised that Moray and the exiled rebels would be pardoned and allowed to return to Scotland, and that the Protestant faith would be upheld. In return, he was to receive the crown matrimonial of Scotland which would make him King by law if Mary died without issue. The first stage of the conspiracy was to get rid of the threat of Rizzio by murdering him, and in this Darnley was to

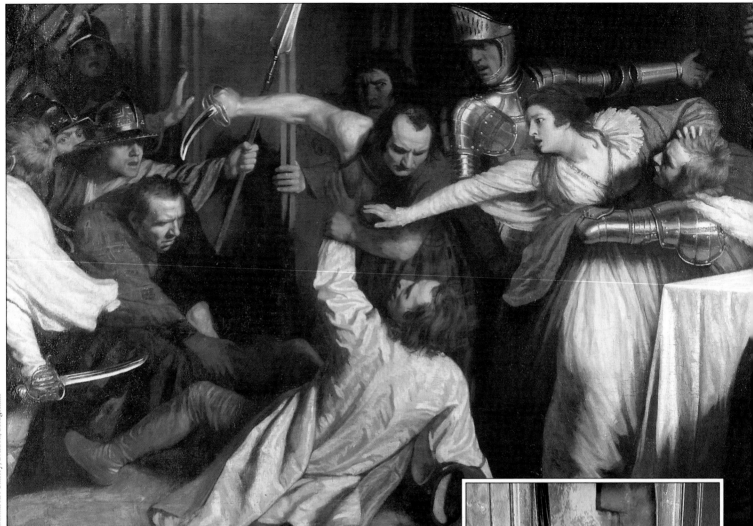

Guildhall Art Gallery, London/Bridgeman

By Gracious Permission of HM the Queen

play a key role: even though he did not actually stab the victim, his dagger was left by the body to prove his complicity in the murder. With Holyrood surrounded by conspirators, there was no chance for the Queen and her supporters to escape. For the first – but not the last – time in her life, Mary became a prisoner. Meanwhile, Moray and his Protestant supporters rode into Edinburgh.

Even more improbable was the next step in this drama. Mary, although hysterical, quickly managed to compose herself and began to think about revenge. The next day she persuaded Darnley to join her, either by flattery or sexual wiles, or by convincing him that his chances under the new regime were little better than under hers. Within 24 hours of the murder, Darnley, who had just betrayed Mary to the Protestant lords, had become her beloved husband, anxious to do her bidding and prepared to reveal the names of his recent confederates in crime. Two days later, the Queen and the treacherous Darnley escaped to the Earl of Bothwell's castle at Dunbar, the heavily pregnant Mary enduring the five-hour flight on horseback with remarkable courage and determination.

🕮 *Rizzio's murder took place on 9 March 1566. While Mary was dining in her private chambers with a small company of courtiers, including Rizzio, Darnley entered, greeted his wife affectionately and joined the guests. Darnley's entry into the supper party was the signal for his fellow conspirators to burst in, drag Rizzio away and stab him to death in an adjoining room. But at this dramatic moment, Mary intervened, pleading with Darnley until he was forced to hold her back* above. *Then, according to Mary, 'They dragged David with great cruelty forth from our cabinet and at the entrance of our chamber dealt him 56 dagger wounds.' On Darnley's command, the body was thrown down a staircase* right *and dragged into the porter's lodge. There is little doubt that one of the intentions of the murderers was to threaten the lives of Mary and her unborn child*

National Portrait Gallery, London

JAMES

Although Mary and Darnley's marriage ended in disaster, the child born of their union enjoyed a fate very different from that of his parents, for as James VI of Scotland and James I of England he would unite the two kingdoms, his mother's claims to which had caused her tragic death.

James never knew his father, and merely corresponded with his mother throughout her imprisonment in England. Amid all the bloodshed and turmoil in his own kingdom, the news of his mother's execution seems to have affected him hardly at all. James grew up a strange man, asserting that he was King by the Grace of God and that no man could take away his divine right to rule. For all his oddities that earned him the title of the 'Wisest Fool in Christendom', he was a gentle and pacific ruler, preferring books to warfare

festivities. He had incurred the scorn and hatred not merely of Mary but also of the Scottish nobles. Predictably, Darnley responded to these slights by foolishly and publicly complaining of his grievances. To further prove his point, he absented himself from his son's christening, although he was actually in the castle at the time.

In October Mary fell seriously ill in Jedburgh. Yet, although she came close to death at one point, Darnley did not visit her until 11 days after she fell ill, and he stayed only briefly. 'He misuses himself so far towards her that it is a heartbreak for her to think that he should be her husband,' wrote Lethington. Mary now knew that she must make an irrevocable break with Darnley.

Deepening depression

By December her depression had deepened. 'The Queen is not well,' the French Ambassador wrote, 'but I think the real cause of her illness is a sorrow which she cannot forget. Again and again she says, "Oh that I could die!"' He further commented that in future no understanding could be expected between Mary and Darnley for two reasons: 'The first is, the King will never humble himself as he ought: the other is the Queen cannot observe any nobleman speaking with the King, but that she at once suspects some contrivance between them.' The brief, intense love affair between Mary Stuart and Lord Darnley was over.

With Bothwell's help, Mary gathered enough support to defeat the opposition. Rizzio's murderers fled to England, Moray and his friends withdrew from Edinburgh and, on 18 March, less than ten days after the murder, Mary made a triumphant re-entry into the capital.

Relations between Mary and Darnley now settled into an uneasy truce while the Queen awaited the birth of her child. On 19 June 1566 Mary was delivered of a healthy son. The news was greeted with immense rejoicing in Edinburgh. As she presented the child to Darnley, she announced publicly, 'My lord, God has given you and me a son, begotten by none but you...for he is so much your own son that I fear it will be the worse for him hereafter.' With this utterance – and the contemptuous aside – Mary hoped to remove any threat of illegitimacy that might result from a future divorce. The child was christened James after his grandfather.

Love turned to loathing

At the time of Rizzio's murder Mary had stated that she could 'forgive but not forget' Darnley's complicity in the affair, but this was easier said than done. Her love for her husband had turned to disdain and finally loathing; her detestation of him was partly a detestation of her own mistake. The prospect of the intimacies of marriage, which would have to be resumed soon after the birth, seemed not merely distasteful but insupportable. She and her advisers talked of a divorce but they suggested it be in the future, so as to safeguard the legitimacy of her heir. In the meantime, Mary had to bide her time.

Darnley, now powerless and isolated, was aware that he was King in name only. He was no longer summoned to the Council or invited to

⚜ *In 1566, Mary became violently ill at a house in Jedburgh in the Scottish border country* below. *In addition to convulsions and vomiting, she was suffering from severe mental stress and, possibly, post-natal depression*

Edinburgh Photographic Library

THE BEJEWELLED QUEEN

By the end of her life, Mary Queen of Scots had amassed a magnificent collection of jewels. Besides adorning herself with them, she treated them as the financial assets they were, using them as security, giving them as presents or selling them for ready money. One of her most famous pieces to survive the years was a necklace of 37 particularly fine pearls which had been a wedding gift from Catherine de Medici. Queen Elizabeth purchased it, along with other items, after Mary's execution; Elizabeth left it to James I, and it eventually passed to Queen Victoria

By Gracious Permission of HM the Queen

National Library of Scotland

♔The Darnley or Lennox Jewel dates from the 1570s and was made for Margaret Douglas, Darnley's mother, in memory of her husband, the Earl of Lennox, who died in 1571. Made of gold enamelled in various colours and set with a sapphire, rubies and an emerald, the intricate jewel is shaped like a heart and bears various inscriptions, emblems and symbols. The motto on the face *above* translates as 'Who hopes still constantly with patience shall obtain victory in their claim' and refers to Margaret's grandson James. In the centre is a winged heart – the symbol of the Douglas family – topped with a crown and surrounded by four allegorical figures representing Faith, Victory and Truth. The winged heart, the crown and the Darnley Jewel itself all open up to reveal additional symbols and mottoes referring to Margaret's life and that of her family

♔Henry Stuart, Lord Darnley, and Mary Queen of Scots *left*. Darnley, who is wearing a suit of armour, bears a shield with the Darnley coat of arms. This features three lions rampant and several fleurs-de-lis, both common symbols in Scottish Royal arms. The same symbols adorn Mary's underskirt, and in her hand she carries a thistle, the Scottish national emblem

MARIA·D·GRATIA
REGINA·SCOTORV
ÆTATIS·SVÆ·

1583

IACOBVS
DEI·GRATIA
REX·SCOTORV
ÆTATIS·SVÆ·17

♛ Mary and her son James are portrayed in this double portrait *above* painted by an unknown artist in 1583 when James was 17 years old. But since the Queen never saw her son after the first few days of his life, it is clear that one or – more likely – both portraits are copies of existing paintings. The Royal Crown of Scotland, painted between the two likenesses, dates from the time of Mary's father James V, and incorporates the crown of his Stuart ancestors as well as parts of the crown of Robert the Bruce. The crown passed on to Mary, who was crowned when she was only nine months old, then to her son James and her grandson Charles

♛ Two pendants, both of enamelled gold set with stones: the Scottish-made heart-shaped pendant set with a French portrait cameo of the Queen *far left* was, it is believed, one of the jewels given by Mary to her serving-woman, Giles Mowbray, shortly before Mary's execution and collectively known as the Penicuik Jewels. The armorial pendant *left* bears a glass cast of the face of Mary Queen of Scots' signet ring; the setting is probably mid-19th century

THE BEGINNING OF THE END

JUST THREE MONTHS AFTER DARNLEY'S MURDER, MARY MARRIED THE CHIEF SUSPECT. THE QUEEN MAY HAVE BEEN IN FEAR OF HER LIFE, BUT HER STRANGE ACTION SEALED HER DOWNFALL

IN THE SUMMER OF 1566 MARY HAD BROACHED the idea of a divorce from Darnley with her advisers. They agreed to consider the matter, but quietly suggested that there might be 'other means' of getting rid of him. Mary, unwilling to take part in further discussions, left the vexed question of Darnley to Moray and the nobles.

Aware that she could not trust her husband, Mary had pardoned the conspirators in Rizzio's murder, thereby making Darnley's position very vulnerable; his fellow conspirators openly vowed revenge against the traitor. Darnley therefore retreated to Glasgow, his family's stronghold, and it was here that he fell ill – perhaps of smallpox, but more probably of syphilis.

♛ *Mary tried hard to save her marriage but her attempts at reconciliation with her husband below were to no avail. Their relationship got into difficulties very quickly and, after Rizzio's horrifying murder, they were entirely estranged*

Courtesy of Astley House Fine Art, Moreton-in-Marsh, Glos.

Courtesy of the Trustees of the V & A/Bridgeman

♛ **Above** *The Darnley conspirators: a group of aristocrats prepare to murder their king.* **Below right** *A contemporary sketch by an English agent shows Darnley's house reduced to rubble (centre left) by the explosion. The corpses of Darnley and his servant lie in the gardens, still dressed in their nightclothes, and the infant James appears in his cradle (top left), saying 'Judge and avenge my cause, O Lord.' At the bottom of the sketch, the crowd watches Darnley's body being carried away. He was not yet 21 when he was murdered*

'*Albeit we found his doings rude, yet were his words and answers gentle*'

MARY ON BOTHWELL

quarters of a mile from Holyrood. During the week that followed Mary spent much of her time there; Darnley had begged her forgiveness and the two got on remarkably well.

On the evening before Darnley was to rejoin her at Holyrood, Mary left to attend a wedding party and did not return to Kirk o'Field. At two o'clock that night she was woken by a tremendous explosion – as was most of Edinburgh. The house at Kirk o'Field had been blown up and the bodies of Darnley and a servant found in a nearby garden. They had been strangled.

Mystery of Darnley's murder

The question will always remain. Did Mary know about the murder plot or had she deliberately taken care not to enquire?

When the news reached the French and English courts, Elizabeth I and Catherine de Medici both wrote to Mary telling her in the strongest terms that justice must be done, and seen to be done without delay. Yet the chief suspect, the Earl of Bothwell, walked tall in the streets of Edinburgh, consolidating his position as the Queen's trusted adviser.

Soon placards appeared on the walls of Edinburgh denouncing him. The most famous and scurrilous of these implicated Mary as well. She appeared as a mermaid, naked to the waist with a crown on her head – a mermaid in the vulgar symbolism of the times denoted a prostitute. Bothwell was depicted as a hare (his family crest) crouching in a circle of swords. Even after

Whether Mary suspected that Darnley was plotting against her again, this time with the force of the Lennoxes and their friends behind him, is not known. For whatever reason, Mary visited him and persuaded him, with the promise of a reconciliation, to return to Edinburgh with her. She arranged for him to convalesce in the Provost's Lodge at Kirk o'Field, about three-

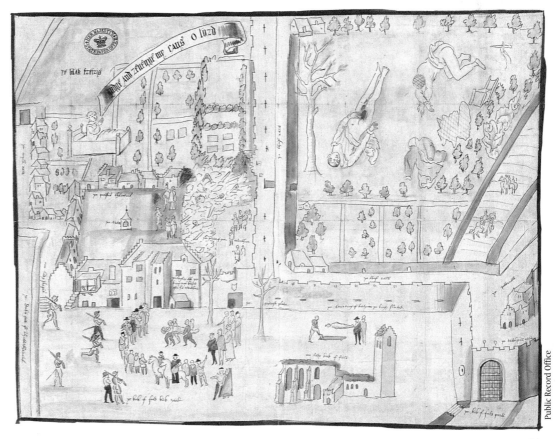

Public Record Office

♛ *The events of 1567 turned public opinion firmly against Mary and sealed her fate. This picture above was painted that year and depicts the newly crowned 13-month-old James VI kneeling at the tomb of his father. Darnley's parents and brother join in the child's prayers for vengeance. The answer to their prayers is recorded in the bottom lefthand corner, which shows the defeat of Bothwell at Carberry Hill*

this outrageous insult Mary did nothing. By now the rumours had reached France. Her ambassador at the French court wrote to her with unusual frankness, 'You yourself have become the object of calumny here, being regarded as having planned and commanded this crime.'

Eventually it was Lennox, Darnley's outraged father, who brought charges against Bothwell. Edinburgh, however, was the seat of Bothwell's power and influence. Lennox was allowed to bring only six of his followers with him to the trial in the capital. Unable to enter the city safely with so small a force, he could not

make his case and Bothwell was acquitted. Around this time Moray declared his intention of leaving Scotland 'to see Venice and Milan', an ominous departure since his disappearance from the political scene always heralded trouble. Mary turned instead for advice to the very man who was reputed to have killed her husband. At the next meeting of the Scottish parliament, Bothwell was given new lands, further evidence of the favour he now enjoyed in the eyes of the Queen. Politically, Mary could hardly have made a more ill-judged move.

Shortly afterwards, when she was travelling

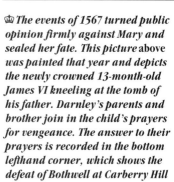

ELIZABETH I

While Mary gained notoriety through the scandals attached to her marriages, her cousin, Elizabeth of England, was remarkable for the fact that she never married at all. Her claim to have been the 'Virgin Queen', however, was probably not strictly accurate – Robert Dudley, Earl of Leicester, for one, was almost certainly her lover.

Although they never met, it is possible that Elizabeth developed a sneaking affection – and respect – for Mary through their correspondence, since the Scottish Queen was always forthright in her opinions and the expression of her feelings. But Elizabeth's attitude to her 'good sister and cousin' was highly ambivalent because of the vexed question of religion and the succession to the English throne. Henry VIII's will barred his great-niece from inheriting the crown, but in the eyes of her Catholic neighbours Elizabeth herself was illegitimate, with no right of inheritance. She had made it known that this vital signature would have to be obtained by a trick, as she could not bring herself knowingly to condemn a fellow Queen to death. So her ministers 'hid' the document among a pile of routine papers and thus, in 1587, Elizabeth I signed the death warrant for her cousin Queen Mary of Scotland. After hearing the news of the execution, she suffered terrible anguish and, in her anger and guilt, attempted to transfer the blame onto her unfortunate advisers

National Galleries of Scotland

to Edinburgh from Linlithgow, Bothwell met her on the way. He had with him a force of 800 men, greatly outnumbering her small party. He turned her horse round and docilely she allowed him to lead her to his castle at Dunbar.

Rape of the Queen

Once there Bothwell completed the formal abduction of her person by the physical possession of her body. His purpose was obvious: he wanted a crown and he did not shrink from rape as a means to this end. As Melville, who was in the castle at the time, recounted, 'The Queen could not but marry him, seeing he had ravished her and laid with her against her will.'

Before the marriage could take place, Bothwell had to divorce his wife, Lady Jean Gordon. Mary herself restored the legal jurisdiction of the Archbishop of St Andrews. The helpful bishop declared the marriage null and void and the divorce went through in four days. A triumphant Bothwell led Mary into Edinburgh and on 15 May, 12 days after his divorce and three months after Darnley's murder, the two were married according to Protestant ritual.

A bizarre lover

James Hepburn, Earl of Bothwell, was about five feet six inches tall and described by some as hideously ugly, 'like an ape in purple'. His portrait shows us a swarthy man with a crooked nose and full, sensuous lips, combined with a muscular, well-formed body. He had an animal-like virility and savagery which made him powerfully attractive to women, and he was notoriously dissolute. Described by one contemporary as 'high

'*Repentance has already begun...I noticed something strange in the manner of her and her husband which she sought to excuse*'

THE FRENCH AMBASSADOR ON MARY AND BOTHWELL

♚ *No sooner had Bothwell and Mary entered Bothwell Castle* below *than it was surrounded by angry rebel lords and they were forced to flee again*

♚ *Though not conventionally handsome, James, 4th Earl of Bothwell* top *had a powerful attraction for women. A Norwegian woman named Anna Throndsen left her husband and property to follow him back to Scotland, but Bothwell drew a sharp line between sex and marriage. He eventually married Jean Gordon* above, *the wealthy sister of the powerful Earl of Huntly, divorcing her in 1567 in order to marry the Queen*

Mary Evans Picture Library

seen the throne within his grasp, he proceeded ruthlessly to take what he wanted.

Although it is probable that Mary and Bothwell were not in love, it is obvious that they desperately needed each other: she, because she believed he was the only strong, loyal supporter who could help her save her throne; he, because she had the power to make him king consort and effective ruler of the country. But of all Mary's foolish deeds, her third marriage was the most disastrous yet. It caused the political tide to turn against her and led directly to her downfall.

Mary's unhappiness

On the afternoon of the wedding day, the French ambassador visited her and found her in despair. 'Repentance has already begun,' he reported to Paris. 'When I went to see Her Majesty . . . I noticed something strange in the manner of her and her husband which she sought to excuse; saying that if she was sad, it was because she wished to be so, and she never wished to rejoice again. All that she wished for was death.'

Alas, the effect of Mary's marriage to Bothwell was to unite the Scottish nobles against them, even Maitland of Lethington, one of her most loyal and constant supporters; he quietly rode off to join the rebels. A few days later Mary and Bothwell managed to flee to Dunbar where they gathered together their supporters. And on 15 June 1567 they and their forces met the rebel lords at Carberry Hill just east of Edinburgh.

At Carberry Hill the rebel banner showed a

♛ A 19th-century painting shows Mary at Carberry Hill above. In fact, there was no true battle; the Royal troops melted away and Mary gave herself up to the rebel lords while Bothwell fled, after only five weeks of power. He was outlawed and forced eventually to Norway, where a vengeful Anna Throndsen ensured that her faithless lover spent the rest of his life in prison

in his conceit, proud, vicious and vainglorious without measure, one who would attempt anything out of ambition,' Bothwell came from a powerful noble family that had traditionally defended the Crown. Though a Protestant, he had been loyal to Mary of Guise and, in the early years of Mary's reign, firmly committed to her cause. Political acumen was hardly his strong point, since Bothwell was primarily a soldier who was apt to choose a quick, if violent, solution to any problem. Rough and bullying, he believed that force was the only law and, having

THE CASKET LETTERS

By permission of the Duke of Hamilton and Brandon

The story of the discovery of the Casket Letters may be as true or as false as the letters themselves. These controversial documents were 'found' in June 1567 when one of Bothwell's servants, returning to Edinburgh to fetch his master's clothes, was captured and, under torture, revealed the presence of a silver casket containing correspondence from Mary Stuart to Bothwell. This was handed to the Earl of Morton who formally opened the casket, presumably read the letters and then resealed the casket. However, he made no record of the contents of the letters and stated only that they related to Bothwell. At this stage, the Queen's name was not mentioned at all, nor was the handwriting identified in any way.

It was not until December 1568 that the existence of the letters was made known publicly. The letters were used during Mary's 'trial' at York to prove that she had committed adultery with Bothwell and connived in Darnley's death. It is virtually certain, but now impossible to prove, that most of these 21 assorted documents – there were poems as well as letters – were forged, probably by Morton and Moray. None of the letters presented as evidence at the trial were originals – they were all copies, many being translations into English from the 'original' French; none, moreover, were signed or dated. Mary vehemently denied the authorship of these letters, which she was never allowed to see

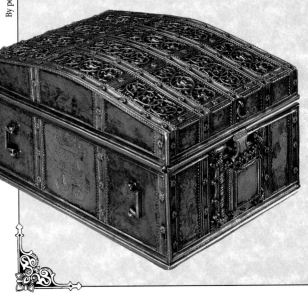

green tree against a white ground, with Darnley's corpse beneath it and baby Prince James kneeling beside it. Across it was written: 'Judge and avenge my cause, O Lord.' In the parleys that were held, Mary angrily refused to leave her husband and jeopardize the legitimacy of her unborn child. In the interests of peace she gave herself up to the rebel lords who promised to conduct her to Edinburgh with all due honour.

Imprisonment and abdication

Mary was imprisoned on the island of Lochleven, where just over a month later she suffered a miscarriage of twins. Still not completely broken, she enlisted the help of Elizabeth I, who, in a remarkable gesture of support, fiercely reproved the lords for their presumptuous action; there was no law, she pointed out, that authorized them to hold Mary prisoner.

At this point came the fortuitous discovery of the infamous Casket Letters, allegedly written by Mary herself, implicating her beyond doubt in the plot with Bothwell and others to murder Darnley. It was precisely the 'proof' the lords wanted. Now they could compel Mary 'of her own free will' to make over the Crown to her son. If she refused, they would publicly accuse her of adultery and of being an accessory to her husband's murder.

Mary signed her act of abdication on 25 July 1567. Her son was crowned King of Scotland a few days later and the Earl of Moray returned in triumph to be appointed Regent.

☙ *By the 19th century, Mary's downfall had become heavily romanticized, though at the time her enemies blackened her name as much as they could. The painting left of Mary's return to Edinburgh after the defeat at Carberry Hill shows nothing of the placards and bills which had plastered the town, deriding the Queen as a whore who had married her husband's murderer. The soldiers insulted her crudely, calling for her to be burned or drowned, and the Edinburgh crowd hurled abuse. With tears of shock and humiliation streaming down her cheeks, Mary realized she had truly lost the love of her people. She was incarcerated in the grim, dank castle of Lochleven the following day. A few weeks later, alone, friendless and surrounded by soldiers, Mary was called from the bed where she had just miscarried of twins to sign her abdication right. She was 24 years old*

Mansell

✠King James VI *right* fulfilled his mother's ambition when he succeeded to the English throne as James I and, with his wife Anne of Denmark *above*, founded the first Royal Family to unite the kingdoms of England and Scotland. It was a political match and James did not meet his bride until four months after his proxy had married her in Copenhagen in August 1589. Anne was on her way to Scotland when adverse winds forced her voyage to a halt. The solemn, bookish young King had already fallen in love from afar with the lively Danish Princess and he set out himself to meet her in Oslo. Anne was only 16 and James 23, yet their love endured and they went on to have seven children

👑Elizabeth of Bohemia *above* was Mary's only surviving granddaughter and the wife of Frederick V, Elector Palatine of the Rhine. As a child she was unknowingly a key figure in the famous 'Gunpowder Plot': Guy Fawkes and his associates intended to place her on the throne as a puppet queen, after killing her parents and brothers and converting the nine-year-old Princess to Catholicism. Her daughter Sophia married the Elector of Hanover and was the mother of George I

👑James's eldest son Henry, Prince of Wales *above right*, was born in 1593, and grew into a highly intelligent and fearless young man who made a strong impression on all who met him. Henry was enormously popular and the whole country went into mourning when he died at 18 from typhoid. He and Princess Elizabeth were very close; his last words before dying were 'Where is my dear sister?'

👑'When I am King, you shall be Archbishop of Canterbury.' So Henry is said to have spoken to his younger brother. But the death of Henry meant that Charles, the frail and sickly Duke of York *right*, became the heir. Charles was then 12 years old, a shy and solemn boy whose reign as Charles I would plunge the nation into civil war and end in his own execution: history was repeated when he died as his grandmother had died

A LIFE REMEMBERED

As Mary Queen of Scots knelt before the block in the great hall of Fotheringhay Castle and prepared to die, thoughts of the people and things she had most loved must have passed through her mind: her three husbands, sickly Francis, ruthless Bothwell and, above all, handsome Darnley...places she had thought of as home, if only for a little while...loyal followers and friends...her child. Then came the fatal blow and the tragic Queen was no more

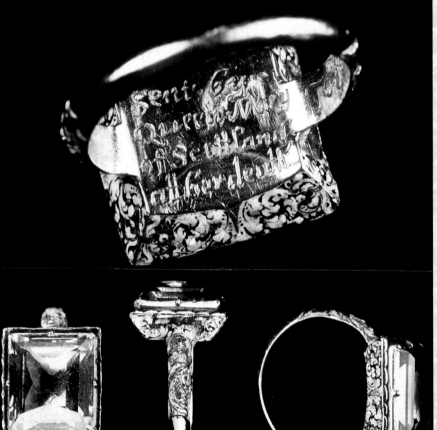

The Ceylon sapphire ring *above* is made of enamelled gold set with a large sapphire. It was sent to John Hamilton – Abbot of Paisley and Archbishop of St Andrews as well as keeper of the privy seal and lord treasurer – after Mary's execution. Hamilton, a loyal supporter of the Queen, was hanged in 1571 for complicity in the murders of Darnley and Moray

Edinburgh Photographic Library

♛Magnificent Stirling Castle *left* was to be a haven of safety and a source of happy memories to Mary throughout her life. The initials MR (for Maria Regina) are carved into the ramparts at the place where the young Queen liked to rest, known as Queen Mary's look-out. The castle's massive granite walls sheltered the Royal baby from the threat of English kidnappers and, at just nine months old, she was crowned Queen in the Chapel Royal there. Many years later, when she had returned from France, the stern old castle witnessed the sudden flowering of love between two young cousins as Mary nursed Darnley devotedly through the long days of his illness. By the following year the marriage was in a bad way, but the one product of the union, the infant James, was given a splendid formal baptism at Stirling in December 1566, followed the next day by a bull hunt, a banquet and a masque. The last time Mary saw her child was at the castle a few months later, when James was less than a year old

♛There are few contemporary portraits of Mary and Darnley; the painting *below* is the only surviving portrait of the Queen painted during her reign in Scotland

♛The 'Darnley ring' *left* bears the lovers' joint initials – HM – and a rope design on the front. On the inside are Darnley's arms, his name and the date, 1565, which was also the year of Mary and Darnley's wedding. The ring was reputedly found at Fotheringhay Castle. For a long time it was believed to be entirely authentic, but it is now thought that the initials have been altered, and that the engravings on the inside of the ring are 19th-century additions

National Trust Photo Library

FINAL INDIGNITIES

EIGHTEEN YEARS OF IMPRISONMENT DID NOT BREAK MARY'S AMBITION. DRIVEN BY HER LIFELONG DREAM – TO TAKE THE ENGLISH CROWN – SHE WAS DRAWN INTO MANY PLOTS, BUT MET HER FINAL HOUR AS BEFITS A QUEEN

BY THE AUTUMN OF 1567 MARY HAD REGAINED some of her old spirit. Her prison at Lochleven was a gloomy stronghold on an island, but from her window she could see across a lovely lake to the forests and mountains of the mainland. She was allowed to walk in the garden; she began to dance once more and take an interest in her clothes; she played cards, she embroidered and she light-heartedly charmed her jailers. One of them, George Douglas, a personable, gallant young nobleman, was soon 'lost in a fantasy of love' for her and, after some months, with his help and that of his plucky young cousin Willy, she was able to escape from the island in May 1568.

Within a week Mary had collected an army of 6000 men as supporters flocked to her.

Although she offered to negotiate with Moray, preferring as always to settle for peace rather than do battle, he refused; he no longer needed or wanted to rule by his half-sister's grace. Their forces met at Langside near Glasgow on 13 May 1568 in a brief but decisive battle. Moray's army, although numerically inferior to Mary's, was better led and better disciplined, and Mary's troops were soundly defeated.

Once more Mary made a disastrous decision at this momentous occasion. Instead of remaining in Scotland (where she could have rallied further support) or going to France (to seek help in the same way) she chose to seek refuge in England. After all, she reasoned, had not Elizabeth written to her in her dark days of imprisonment, 'You can at any time count on my support'? Mary

Sir William Cecil above left, Elizabeth I's principal minister and adviser, never ceased to be on his guard against Mary; he regarded her as a menace to the English throne and to Protestantism. Yet, like so many others, he could not but admire the pride, grace and dignity she displayed right up to the hour of her death right

Mary's escape from Lochleven was complicated by having a lake to cross below, but on 2 May 1568, dressed as a countrywoman, she boldly walked out of the main gate to the waiting boat

NIÆ REGIS MATER, QVAM SVORVM HÆRESI VEXATAM
REBELLIONE OPPRESSAM, REFVGY CAVSA VERBO ELIS
REGINA ET COGNATA INNIXAM IN ANGLIAM AN
1568 DESCENDENTEM · 19 AN CAPTIVAM PER
FIDIA DETINVIT MILLEQ CALVMNYS TRADVXIT
CRVDELI SENATVS ANGLICI SENTENTIA
HÆRESI INSTIGANTE NECI TRADITVR
AC 12 KAL · MART 1587 A SERVILI
CARNIFICE OBTRVNCATVR AN°
ÆTAT REGNIQ · 45

AVLA FODRINGHA MY

REGINAM SERENISS REGVM
FILIAM VXOREM ET MATREM
ASTANTIBVS COMMISSARIIS
ET MINISTRIS R ELI: CAR
NIFEX SECVRI PERCVIT :
ATQ VNO ET ALTERO
ICTV TRVCVLENTER SAV
CIATA TERTIO EI CAPVT
ABSCINDIT

Both National Trust Photo Library

♛ The Earl of Shrewsbury far right and his wife Bess of Hardwick right were to act as Mary's jailers from 1569. Although immensely rich and owner of a vast number of properties, Shrewsbury was obsessed with his account book and constantly worried about the expenses his extravagant prisoner, with her own household of nearly 50 persons, incurred. Bess shared his interest in material possessions but was a much stronger character with a shrewd business sense. The conflicting roles of 'host and hostess' on the one hand, and keepers on the other, responsible for the safety and security of their Royal charge, were often hard to reconcile. Just as difficult for the couple was the question of Mary's social life – her frequent visits to the spa of Buxton below, for example, aroused Queen Elizabeth's suspicion but became Mary's sole pleasure as her health deteriorated. The then fashionable baths of Buxton were famous for their healing powers and attracted courtiers and noblemen from all over the country – a unique chance for Mary to mix with people. Shrewsbury had a special house built for Mary next to the baths where she could take her cure while being closely guarded

therefore crossed the Solway Firth and set foot on English soil for the first time on 16 May.

Mary's brave but foolish and misconceived gesture put Elizabeth in an awkward position. As a ruling Queen herself, she had always supported Mary against any rebels. But her chief minister Cecil regarded her as the arch-enemy of Protestantism and a conspicuous threat to England. Moreover, after it became known that

some of England's leading nobles had paid honour to the fugitive Queen, Elizabeth was even more inclined to listen to Cecil's advice. Mary was therefore officially received and 'interviewed' by Sir Francis Knollys, Elizabeth's vice-chamberlain, at Carlisle Castle. He was impressed by the Queen and wrote to Cecil, 'Surely she is a rare woman for, as no flattery can abuse her, so no plain speech seems to offend her, if

'I would rather die than agree; the last words of my life shall be those of a queen of Scotland'

MARY ON THE POSSIBILITY OF ABDICATING

she think the speaker an honest man.' But he was obliged to tell Mary that she could not be received at the English Court until she had been purged of the stain of her husband's murder.

Thus, within five months of her reception by Knollys, Mary found herself on trial at York for the crimes alleged against her by Moray and the Scottish lords, the evidence of which was contained in the Casket Letters. Whether the trial or 'conference' (as it was euphemistically called) had any legal validity is doubtful and, mindful of this, the English authorities were careful to pass

Spectrum

neither verdict nor sentence. Throughout it, Mary was resolute and determined, declaring that the Casket Letters were forged and, further, that she had abdicated under duress. On the possibility of renouncing the Crown, she declared, 'I would rather die than agree; the last words of my life shall be those of a queen of Scotland.'

In the end, however, the York trial concluded that Mary should remain in England and Moray should retain his position as Scotland's Regent. Mary Stuart became, therefore, not so much Elizabeth's guest as her prisoner – and was to remain so for 18 long years.

Bothwell's fate

After the defeat at Carberry, Bothwell had fled initially to Orkney, then to Shetland and finally to Norway, where he was captured and arraigned for breach of promise by his former mistress, Anna Throndsen. King Frederick of Denmark and Norway, perceiving Bothwell's usefulness as a political pawn, then incarcerated him in a series of fortress prisons, refusing all extradition requests from Moray. Trial in Scotland and even death might have been preferable to what this once strong and vigorous man endured, which was 11 years of solitary confinement in a tiny cell. In the end, he was driven insane and,

SHEFFIELD CASTLE

Of her 18 years in captivity, Mary spent 15 years in Sheffield under the custody of Lord Shrewsbury, with her time divided between the town's fortress – Sheffield Castle – and Sheffield Manor, which was about a mile away, and which the Shrewsburys used as a hunting lodge and summer residence. The propinquity of the two residences solved the cleaning problem as Mary could be shifted from one to the other. Originally built in the 12th century by William de Lovetot, Sheffield Castle was almost entirely demolished during the Civil War in 1648, whereas part of the once-splendid Tudor Manor, the small lodge known as the Turret House, is still perfectly preserved. As the latter was built during Mary's captivity in Sheffield, it has been suggested that the Turret House had been specifically designed as a prison for her. Its richly decorated upper rooms, known as Queen Mary's Rooms, support this theory, as does the fact that there was only one (easily guarded) entrance to the building. The Turret House now houses a small museum

'overgrown with hair and filth', he died.

Mary began her first long term of imprisonment in 1570, just before her 28th birthday, as a 'guest' of George Talbot, Earl of Shrewsbury, one of the richest men in the kingdom and bearer of one of the oldest and most respected titles in England. He was married to one of the most formidable women of the 16th century, Bess of Hardwick, and soon after Mary joined the

⚜ Even though all Mary's correspondence was supposed to pass through Shrewsbury's hands, her secret wheeling and dealing, conspiracies, schemes, and codes remained a constant problem to Elizabeth, who frequently summoned her counsellors to give her emergency advice below

By permission of His Grace the Duke of Norfolk

Ancient Art and Architecture Collection

👑 *Thomas Howard, Duke of Norfolk* above, *a wealthy and powerful nobleman (his Shield of Arms is shown* left*), was the central figure in the Ridolfi Plot. Had it succeeded, Mary and Elizabeth's roles would have been exchanged – the Duke would have married Mary, Elizabeth would have been murdered or imprisoned, and Mary and her consort would have ascended to the throne of England. But the discovery of the plot led to Norfolk's execution and precipitated Mary's downfall*

Shrewsbury household, the two women struck up a notable friendship.

Mary spent the next 14 years of her life at Sheffield, with occasional visits to the fashionable spa at Buxton and to Chatsworth, the splendid Derbyshire house built by Bess. Although effectively in captivity, Mary was not uncomfortable. She lived in the elegant surroundings of a home decorated with French furniture and paintings and, as dowager Queen of France, she drew an income of £12,000 (worth several million today), with which she maintained her secretariat and a large diplomatic network in Europe, while presiding over her own household of 50 people.

A comfortable prison

Mary was able to ride in the countryside, make music, hold and attend small banquets, view the hunt and, in the company of Bess of Hardwick, stitch elaborate and exquisite embroideries. She was able to have an aviary and a dovecot, and to import from France the tiny lapdogs she liked so much.

Yet throughout these long years Mary remained a constant problem to Elizabeth I. Her ministers, particularly Cecil and Sir Francis Walsingham, believed that as long as this Catholic rival was alive, she posed a threat to Protestantism and to the Queen herself.

Mary, of course, did not help matters. Since she regarded herself as a sovereign Queen over whom Elizabeth had no jurisdiction – and consequently as illegally held – she considered herself free to try to achieve her liberty by any means in her power. Coded letters and documents were passed back and forth across the Continent, to Scotland and to wherever her supporters were. Mary plotted ceaselessly, looking for help from wherever she could find it.

Plans to marry the Duke of Norfolk – England's premier Duke, who was also a Roman Catholic – were scotched when Elizabeth heard of the scheme and angrily threw Norfolk into the Tower of London. As it so happened, Mary and Norfolk never actually met and the negotiations were carried out by correspondence.

The Ridolfi Plot

A more dangerous conspiracy with which Mary was at least partially involved was a scheme devised by an Italian banker in London, Roberto Ridolfi. His aim was apparently to secure an invasion of England from the Spanish Netherlands led by the Spanish General, the Duke of Alva. The invading forces would be joined by Catholic rebels in England and together they would seize Elizabeth I, then place Mary with her consort Norfolk on the throne. This hare-brained, unrealistic plot was, of course, discovered, with the result that in June 1572 Norfolk was tried and executed for high treason.

Nor was Mary to escape. With incriminating letters written by her to the conspirators in their hands, the English Government now turned completely against her. This 'monstrous dragon' was seen as a Catholic foreigner on English soil whose intrigues were aimed at the overthrow of a Protestant queen in favour of herself and the re-establishment of Catholicism in England. When Parliament met in Westminster in 1572 to decide her fate, Mary received the full brunt of their hatred as members urged that her head be cut off

By Gracious Permission of HM the Queen

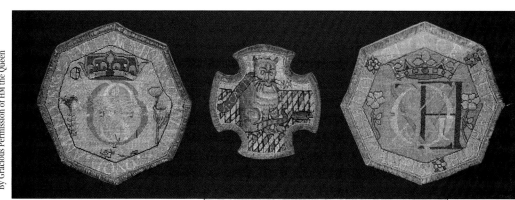

Mary Evans Picture Library

♛ *Tutbury Castle in Staffordshire below was just one of many residences in which Mary was temporarily lodged during her captive years. The gloomy, damp and draughty stronghold became her most hated prison. It was from here that she started her fatal communications with the reckless Thomas Babington – by messenger pigeon* left *when all other means failed. A 25-year-old Catholic squire, Babington was determined to liberate Mary, whom he greatly admired. He managed to gather together a circle of co-conspirators but foolishly outlined every detail of his plot in a letter to Mary. Had she not responded to the letter, the course of history might have been different. But her reply found its way into Walsingham's hands and, finally, sealed her fate*

MARY'S EMBROIDERIES

Embroidery was one of the great comforts of Mary's life during captivity, and especially during her long period at Sheffield Castle. Many of the splendid pieces which date from this time were executed jointly with Bess of Hardwick, the two women idling away the hours in a hobby which amounted to almost a passion with Mary. Some of their embroidery work can be seen to this day at Oxburgh Hall in Norfolk.

In the numerous bedhangings, chair covers and panels, Mary seems to have recorded much of her own life, imaginatively and skilfully weaving motifs, emblems and mottoes into them which were remembrances of times past. One, for example, depicted a phoenix in flames, said to be the emblem of Mary of Guise, and the accompanying words were Mary's famous motto, *En ma fin est mon commencement.* Most touching of all, the Greek letter Phi and the letter M, for Francis and Mary, were woven into at least four of the Oxburgh tapestries – more than ten years after the death of Francis

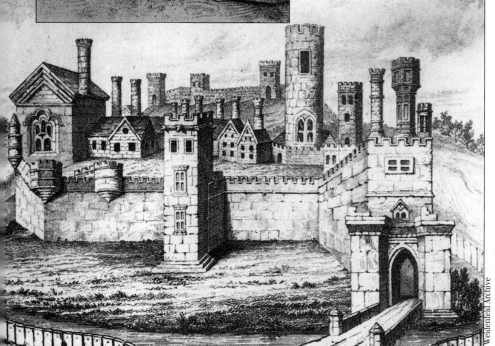

Weidenfeld Archive

'and no more ado made about her'.

Elizabeth did not consent to Mary's execution and Mary remained a captive until 1586 when, prematurely aged and desperate, she was drawn into another plot (possibly devised by Sir Francis Walsingham as a trap), led by a rich, romantic and rather foolish young man, Thomas Babington. The rather vague scheme, like all the others, was designed to liberate Mary, re-establish Catholicism and assassinate Elizabeth, but so ludicrous were the plans that Mary's secretary advised her not to read them. But she did, and in a series of letters to Babington – which found their way into Walsingham's hands – she signed her own death warrant.

She was brought to trial in the Great Hall at Fotheringhay, a castle in Northamptonshire. Although ill and limping badly, she defended herself with remarkable courage and dignity, but had little chance of proving her innocence. She was sentenced to death – though it took Elizabeth three months to sign the death warrant, which she finally did with evident reluctance.

Musée des Beaux-Arts, Tourcoing/Giraudon/Bridgeman

THE EXECUTION

Mary showed no signs of terror or astonishment when, on 7 February 1587, she was handed the death warrant and told that the execution was to take place the following day. 'In the name of God,' she said, 'these tidings are welcome, and I bless and pray Him that the end of all my bitter sufferings is at hand.' She made only two requests; that her chaplain should assist her to the last; and that she might have more time to prepare herself for death. Both were rejected.

Never did Mary dress more carefully than for this last moment of her life. She chose a formal

⚜ Mary faced the moment she had to go to her death above without the faintest sign of fear. She had chosen her last outfit carefully: a black satin dress embroidered with black velvet, whose train was so long that it had to be carried by her master of the household. Underneath she wore a crimson petticoat – the colour of blood and of Catholic martyrdom. Mary's final term of imprisonment under her new jailer, Sir Amias Paulet right, may have had something to do with her willingness to die, as his harsh regime turned her hitherto privileged existence into the strictest possible confinement

Mansell

Warrant to Execute Mary Stuart, Queen of Scots, A.D. 1587.

Elizabeth R

'In the name of God, these tidings are welcome, and I . . . pray Him that the end of all my bitter sufferings is at hand'

MARY ON RECEIVING HER DEATH WARRANT

🕮 *Despite Elizabeth's reluctance to carry out the death sentence and her repeated plea to Parliament to substitute 'an act for an axe', she finally gave in to pressure and signed Mary's death warrant above, three months after the Fotheringhay trial. It was delivered to Mary on 7 February 1587*

🕮 *The scene of Mary's execution was the Great Hall at Fotheringhay Castle below, where a wooden scaffold, about 12 feet square, had been erected the night before*

robe of state made of black velvet stamped with gold. A white veil reaching to her feet was placed over her wig and she carried two rosaries and a fine white lawn handkerchief with which her eyes were to be bound. Knowing that on the scaffold she would be partially undressed, she chose a petticoat and camisole of crimson velvet.

After praying for two hours, she was led to the Great Hall by the English Lords. She moved with difficulty and pleaded that she might be accompanied to the scaffold by 'six of her best beloved men and women' who had been forbidden to help her beyond her chamber. This final request was allowed. Witnesses, of which there were some 300, report that Mary looked calm, almost joyful, as she mounted the scaffold which was draped in black. She refused the ministrations of a Protestant clergyman who nevertheless recited prayers for her in English. But in clear, ringing tones, she raised her voice against his, intoning the Latin prayers of her own Church. As her black robe was removed, Mary exhorted her assistants not to weep too loudly.

Dignified to the last and with no sign of fear, Mary laid her head on the block. The first blow of

Mansell

Den VIII february werde onthalst Maria Stuart Schot ...

By permission of His Grace the Duke of Norfolk and the Baroness Herries

👑 *The night before her execution Mary made her will and carefully distributed her remaining belongings among servants and friends. The gold rosary and prayer book left which she took to her execution were to be given to her friend Anne Dacres, wife of Philip, Earl of Arundel. All the other objects and pieces of clothing associated with Mary's death were ordered to be burned by the authorities as otherwise they might have become holy relics or items of devotion*

👑 *The serene and composed features of Mary's death mask below convey none of the sufferings, humiliations and ill-health of the Queen's final years. Nor does the almost girlish face show signs of the premature ageing that some of her contemporaries claimed they could see. In fact, the mask matched many a later legend surrounding her – from that of a romantic heroine to that of an innocent martyr*

the axe only cut into the back of her neck. 'Sweet Jesus,' her women heard her whisper. The second blow severed her neck – and was followed by a ghoulish touch of horror. The executioner, wishing to show the head to the audience, gripped it by the hair – Mary's wig. The head dropped to the ground and to the consternation of the assembly rolled like a ball across the scaffold. A deathly silence fell on the hall, broken only a few moments later by the shout of 'God Save the Queen.'

As the body was hurriedly borne away, there was a small but touching scene. Unnoticed, Mary's little dog had crept under her petticoats and now, as it saw its mistress's corpse being carried away, would not leave it until finally, wimpering, it was wrenched away by force.

A legend is born

Mary had once embroidered on a tapestry the words *En ma fin est mon commencement* (in my end is my beginning) – and so it was. The bloody event provoked a wave of indignation all over Catholic Europe; Elizabeth even pretended that the deed itself, as opposed to the sentence, had been done without her consent. The legend of Mary Queen of Scots had already begun, for in death Mary was transformed into a martyr and a romantic, innocent, even saintly figure. The truth, as always, lay somewhere in between.

By permission of the Duke of Hamilton and Brandon

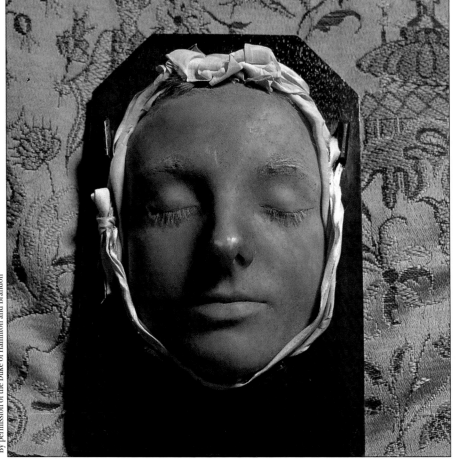